W9-BXY-755

NEW YORK JETS

JETS

BY BARRY WILNER

Published by The Child's World®
1980 Lookout Drive • Mankato, MN 56003-1705
800-599-READ • www.childsworld.com

Acknowledgments
The Child's World®: Mary Berendes, Publishing Director
Red Line Editorial: Editorial direction
The Design Lab: Design
Amnet: Production

Design Element: Dean Bertoncelj/Shutterstock Images
Photographs ©: Perry Knotts/AP Images, cover;
Rich Graessle/Icon Sportswire, 5; Kevin Terrell/AP
Images, 7; Vernon Biever/AP Images, 9; Miami Herald/
ZumaPress/Icon Sportswire, 11; Ric Tapia/Icon
Sportswire, 13; Mark Lennihan/AP Images, 14-15;
Al Messerschmidt Archive/AP Images, 17; Chris Szagola/
Cal Sport Media/Newscom, 19; Anthony J. Causi/Icon
Sportswire, 21; Michael Dwyer/AP Images, 23; Rich Kane/
Icon Sportswire, 25; Damian Strohmeyer/AP Images, 27;
William P. Smith/AP Images, 29

ISBN 9781631439902
LCCN 2014959660

Printed in the United States of America
Mankato, MN
July, 2015
PA02265

ABOUT THE AUTHOR

Barry Wilner has written more than 40 books, including many for young readers. He is a sports writer for the Associated Press and has covered such events as the Super Bowl, Olympics, and World Cup. He lives in Garnerville, New York.

TABLE OF CONTENTS

GO, JETS!

The New York Jets had a humble start. They began play in 1960 in the new American Football League (AFL) at an old stadium. Within ten years, they became the best team in pro football. In the following years, they had a decade without a winning season but also made some of the most memorable moments in football history. No matter the Jets' record, their no-quit attitude makes them a great team. Let's meet the New York Jets.

Wide receiver Eric Decker dives between Detroit Lions players for a touchdown on September 28, 2014.

WHO ARE THE JETS?

The New York Jets are a team in the National Football League (NFL). They are one of the 32 teams in the NFL. The NFL includes the American Football Conference (AFC) and the National Football Conference (NFC). The winner of the AFC plays the winner of the NFC in the **Super Bowl**. The Jets play in the East Division of the AFC. The Jets have won one Super Bowl.

Defensive end Muhammad Wilkerson lines up against the Jacksonville Jaguars on December 9, 2012.

WHERE THEY CAME FROM

The Jets joined the AFL in 1960. They were called the Titans at first. They wanted their name to sound bigger than their neighbors, the New York Giants of the NFL. But people did not think the AFL was as good as the NFL. In 1969, the Jets won the Super Bowl over the NFL's Baltimore Colts. It was the AFL's first Super Bowl win. The next year, the AFL and NFL **merged**. This put the Jets and Giants in the same league.

Joe Namath (12) led the Jets to a big win in the Super Bowl after the 1968 season.

WHO THEY PLAY

The New York Jets play 16 games each season. With so few games, each one is important. Every year, the Jets play two games against each of the other three teams in their division: the Buffalo Bills, the New England Patriots, and the Miami Dolphins. The Dolphins and the Jets are big **rivals**. They have played many thrilling games against each other.

Nick Folk (2) kicks a field goal over Miami Dolphins defenders on December 29, 2013.

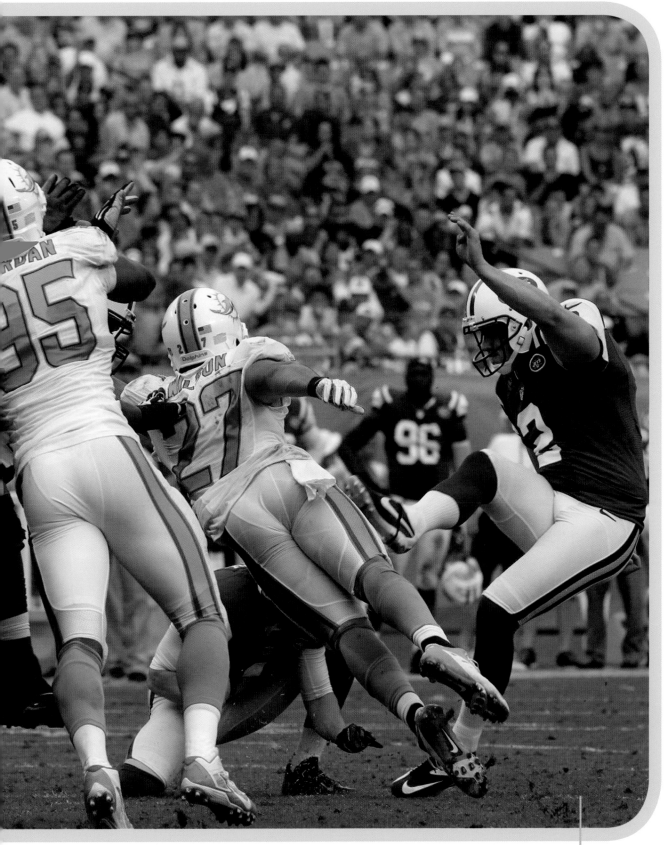

WHERE THEY PLAY

The Jets and New York Giants share MetLife Stadium in New Jersey. It seats 82,500 fans, the most of any stadium in the NFL. MetLife Stadium opened in 2010. In 2014, it hosted the first outdoor Super Bowl in a city with cold weather. The Jets have shared stadiums for a long time. They shared Shea Stadium with baseball's New York Mets from 1964 to 1983. One of the reasons the Jets have their name is because Shea was close to an airport.

MetLife Stadium hosted the Seattle Seahawks and Denver Broncos in the Super Bowl after the 2013 season.

THE FOOTBALL FIELD

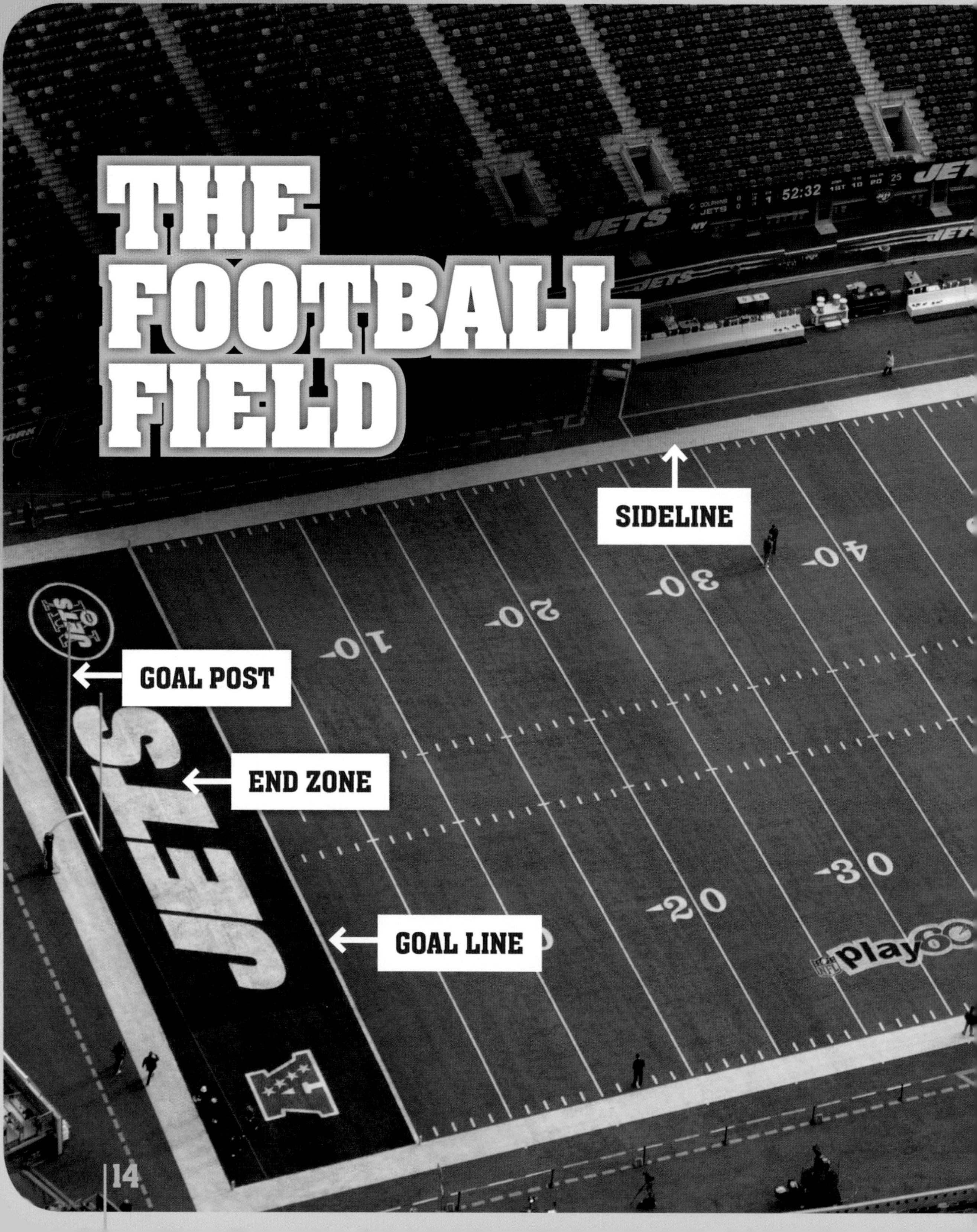

SIDELINE

GOAL POST

END ZONE

GOAL LINE

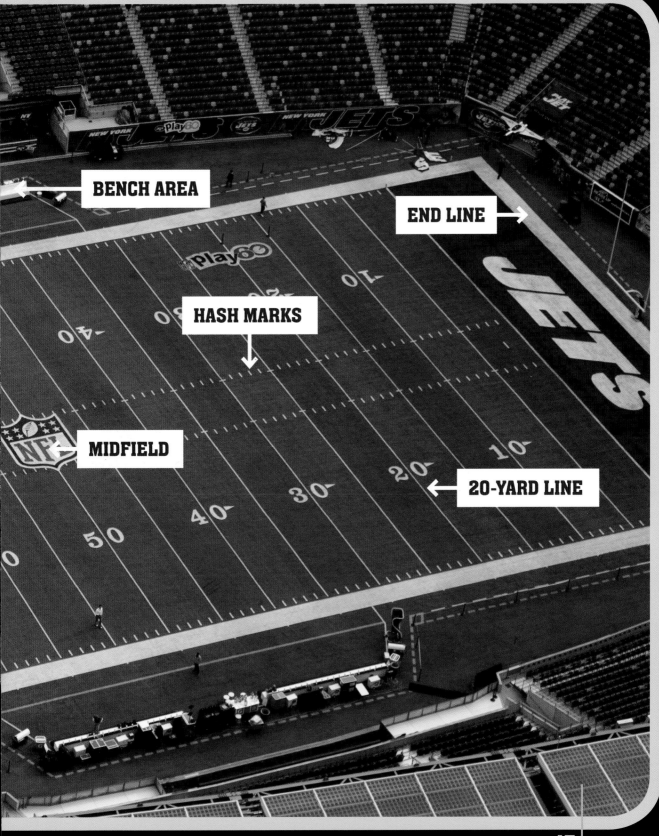

BENCH AREA

END LINE

HASH MARKS

MIDFIELD

20-YARD LINE

BIG DAYS

T he Jets have had some great moments in their history. Here are three of the greatest:

1968—The team went 11-3 and beat the Oakland Raiders for the AFL title. It was the Jets' first time in the playoffs. They were big underdogs for the Super Bowl. But quarterback Joe Namath said the Jets would win. They did. The Jets **upset** the Baltimore Colts on January 12, 1969. They became the first AFL team to win a Super Bowl.

1998—Quarterback Vinny Testaverde led the Jets to a surprising 12-4 regular season record. They beat the Jacksonville Jaguars in the playoffs.

Jumbo Elliott catches his first career touchdown pass and helps the Jets pull off the "Monday Night Miracle."

2000—The Jets trailed the Dolphins 30-7 in the fourth quarter of a *Monday Night Football* game. The Jets made a huge comeback. Tackle Jumbo Elliott caught a **touchdown** with 42 seconds left to force overtime. The Jets then won the game in overtime. The comeback is called the "Monday Night Miracle."

TOUGH DAYS

Football is a hard game. Even the best teams have rough games and seasons. Here are some of the toughest times in Jets history:

1994—In a battle with Miami for first place, the Jets led 24-21 with 30 seconds left. Dolphins quarterback Dan Marino motioned to spike the ball to stop the clock. The Jets players relaxed. Marino faked the spike and threw an easy touchdown to win the game.

1995-1996—The Jets went 3-13 and 1-15 under coach Rich Kotite. These were the worst two seasons in a row in team history.

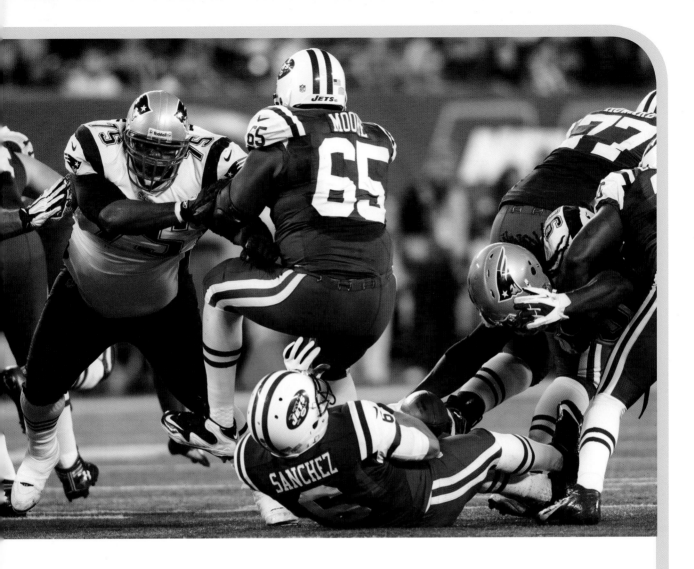

Mark Sanchez (6) fumbles awkwardly against the New England Patriots on Thanksgiving Day 2012.

2012—Against New England, quarterback Mark Sanchez bumped into the rear end of teammate Brandon Moore and dropped the ball. The Patriots' Steve Gregory picked up the ball and scored. The Jets lost 49-19.

MEET THE FANS

Jets fans are known for their cheering. Their chant is one of the most famous in football: "J-E-T-S, Jets, Jets, Jets!" The Jets' most popular fan is Fireman Ed. He led cheers at Jets home games for many years. Today the Jets Flight Crew leads the cheers. Flag carriers fly the green and white team colors around the stadium.

Jets fans cheer on their team during a cold game against the Atlanta Falcons on December 20, 2009.

HEROES THEN

Joe Namath is the Jets' most famous player. "Broadway Joe" led the Jets to their only Super Bowl win. He helped New York fans see the Jets as equal to the Giants. He entered the Pro Football Hall of Fame in 1985. Two years later, Don Maynard joined him in the Hall of Fame. Maynard was Namath's favorite receiver. He was the first player signed by the **franchise**. Running back Curtis Martin entered the Hall of Fame in 2012. He ran for at least 1,000 yards in his first 10 seasons. Only one other player has done this.

Curtis Martin (28) fights for extra yardage on October 15, 2000.

HEROES NOW

Offensive linemen do not always get much attention. But center Nick Mangold has been a star since 2006. He has been to the **Pro Bowl** six times. Jets wide receiver Eric Decker is exciting to watch. He makes many hard catches. On defense, cornerback Darrelle Revis is great at shutting down other teams' wide receivers. And Muhammad Wilkerson is a rising star. He uses strength and speed to get to the other team's quarterback. The Jets have a good kicker, too. Nick Folk almost never misses a **field goal**.

Nick Mangold (74) pushes a defender away from the play on December 8, 2013.

GEARING UP

NFL players wear team uniforms. They wear helmets and pads to keep them safe. Cleats help them make quick moves and run fast. Some players wear extra gear for protection.

THE FOOTBALL

NFL footballs are made of leather. Under the leather is a lining that fills with air to give the ball its shape. The leather has bumps or "pebbles." These help players grip the ball. Laces help players control their throws. Footballs are also called "pigskins" because some of the first balls were made from pig bladders. Today they are made of leather from cows.

Jets wide receiver Jeremy Kerley slips away from a tackle.

HELMET

SHOULDER PADS

THIGH PADS

GLOVES

FOOTBALL

CLEATS

SPORTS STATS

Here are some of the all-time career records for the New York Jets. All the stats are through the 2014 season.

RUSHING YARDS

Curtis Martin 10,302

Freeman McNeil 8,074

PASSING YARDS

Joe Namath 27,057

Ken O'Brien 24,386

TOTAL TOUCHDOWNS

Don Maynard 88

Wesley Walker 71

INTERCEPTIONS

Bill Baird 34

Dainard Paulson 29

SACKS

Mark Gastineau 74

Shaun Ellis 72.5

POINTS

Pat Leahy 1,470

Jim Turner 697

Don Maynard (13) brings in a pass from Joe Namath. Maynard caught 633 passes in his career, a record at the time.

RECEPTIONS

Don Maynard 627

Wayne Chrebet 580

GLOSSARY

field goal a method of scoring worth three points in which a player kicks the ball between the goal posts

franchise a team that is part of a professional sports league

merged when two groups become joined as one

Pro Bowl the NFL's all-star game, in which the best players in the league compete

rivals teams whose games bring out the greatest emotion between the players and the fans on both sides

Super Bowl the championship game of the NFL, played between the winner of the AFC and the NFC

touchdown a method of scoring worth six points in which a player has control of the ball in the other team's end zone

upset when a supposedly weaker team beats a stronger team

FIND OUT MORE

IN THE LIBRARY

Frisch, Aaron. *Super Bowl Champions: New York Jets.*
San Francisco: Chronicle Books, 2014.

Leberfeld, Dan. *Jets Confidential's Book of New York
Jets Trivia.* New York: ASM Publishing, 2009.

Stewart, Mark. *The New York Jets.*
Chicago: Norwood House Press, 2009.

ON THE WEB

Visit our Web site for links about the New York Jets:
childsworld.com/links

*Note to Parents, Teachers, and Librarians: We routinely verify our Web links to make
sure they are safe and active sites. So encourage your readers to check them out!*

INDEX